"*Crafting Your Perfect Picnic Table*"

This book explores the creation of a specific and highly popular style of picnic table, focusing on both design and size. It includes two detailed project plans, both featuring the same design but using different lumber sizes. You'll have the flexibility to choose between two common lumber sizes: 2 x 6 (50 x 150 mm) or 2 x 4 (50 x 100 mm).

The designs showcase sturdy, solid picnic tables with wider tabletops compared to most standard designs.

Build Your Own Eight-Seater Picnic Table

Building with 2 x 4 (50 x 100 mm)
and 2 x 6 (50 x 150 mm) Lumber

By Les Kenny

Les Kenny, 1948–

Build Your Own Eight-Seater Picnic Table

Building with 2 x 4 (50 x 100 mm)
and 2 x 6 (50 x 150 mm) Lumber.

leskenny.com

Table of Contents

Project 1. Using 2x4 (50x100mm) lumber

Table of Contents

Project 2. Using 2x6 (50x150mm) lumber

Project #1

Build Your Own
Eight-Seater Picnic Table

* Using 2 x 4 (50 x 100 mm) lumber

Step-by-step guide

Description

This picnic table is constructed out of 2 x 4 (50 x 100 mm) lumber. It will comfortably seat 8 people. Wide seats positioned both in terms of height and distance from the tabletop ensures easy access and maximum comfort.

Dimensions:
- Length: 8 feet (2.4 m).
- Width: 67" (1700 mm).
- Height: 29⅞" (758 mm).
- Tabletop width: 34¼" (870 mm).

Part identification

[a] Leg	**[e]** Seat board
[b] Middle rail	**[f]** Seat cleat
[c] Top rail	**[g]** Table cleat
[d] Tabletop board	**[h]** Brace

Plans:
Imperial measurements

Below are the picnic table plans, with dimensions given in inches and fractions of an inch.

Plans:
Metric measurements

Below are the picnic table plans, with dimensions given in millimeters.

870 mm

[d]

[e]

[c]

320

720

[b]

400

[a]

1516 mm

150

2.4 m

[g]

[h]

[f]

About the measurements

Length measurements in this project are provided in both imperial units (inches) and metric units (millimeters).

When measurements are presented side by side, the inch measurements are listed first, followed by the metric equivalents in parentheses.

Length example: 15-3/4" (400 mm).

Size example: 2 x 4 (50 x 100 mm), which means that the wood is 2 inches thick and 4 inches wide, or, in metric terms, 50 millimeters thick and 100 millimeters wide.

Abbreviations:

- ": = inch
- ft: = foot, feet
- mm: = millimeter, millimetre
- m: = meter, metre

Shopping list: Lumber

Wood size	Length	Qty
2 x 4 (50 x 100 mm)	8 ft (2.4 m)	24

The lengths provided above are standard stock sizes, which means they are commonly found at major lumber retailers and home improvement centers.

From these listed lengths, you will be able to cut all the pieces required for the construction of the picnic table.

The **cutting plan** shows how to cut all the pieces from the specified lengths to minimize waste.

When purchasing wood for the picnic table, it is advisable to buy dressed lumber, which is wood that has been planed (made smooth).

Shopping list: Fixings

Exterior wood screws:

• 118 screws 3" (75 mm) long.

• 90 screws 3½" (90 mm) long.

1/2" (12 mm) galvanized coach/carriage bolts:

• 12 bolts 4" (100 mm) long.

• 12 each nuts and washers to match.

Note: Use the 3" (75 mm) screws for the frames, cleats, and braces.
Use the 3½" (90 mm) screws for the seat boards and the tabletop boards.

Dressed lumber

Dressed lumber is wood that has been planed and smoothed, which makes it smaller than the nominal sizes given.

For example, 2 x 4 (50 x 100 mm) dressed lumber will be 1½" x 3½" (38 x 89 mm) in actual size.

Different countries and regions may have size variations.

The difference in size will not impact the build as it is the lengths of the pieces that are important, not so much the width and thickness of the wood.

Cutting list

2 x 4 (50 x 100 mm) lumber		
Piece ID	**Length**	**Qty**
[a] Leg	34¾" (883 mm)	6
[b] Middle rail	67" (1700 mm)	3
[c] Top rail	34¼" (870 mm)	3
[d] Tabletop board	8 feet (2.4 m)	9
[e] Seat board	8 feet (2.4 m)	6
[f] Seat cleat	11¼" (285 mm)	4
[g] Table cleat	34¼" (870 mm)	2
[h] Brace	25" (635 mm)	2

[a] ▭ x6
[b] ▭ x3
[c] ▭ x3
[d] ▭ x9
[e] ▭ x6
[f] ▭ x4
[g] ▭ x2
[h] ▭ x2

INSTRUCTIONS

Start the build

Let's go!

Step 1. Cut all the pieces

Cut all the pieces to the lengths given in the **Cutting list**.

All the pieces can be cut from the standard stock lengths that are listed in the **Shopping list**.

Following on the next page is a **Cutting plan** showing how all the pieces can be cut from the standard lengths of lumber given in the **Shopping list**.

from this

cut this

Cutting plan

All the pieces can be cut from the standard stock lengths that are listed in the 'Shopping list'.

The drawing below demonstrates how to cut all the components from the following pieces of 2 x 4 (50 x 100 mm) lumber:

• 24 pieces that are 8 ft (2.4 m) long.

← 8 ft (2.4 m) →	
[d]	x 9
[e]	x 6
[a] [g] [h]	x 2
[a] [a] [f] [f]	x 2
[c] [c]	x 1
[b]	x 3
[c]	x 1

Step 2. Cut the angles

Once all the pieces are cut to length, pieces **[a]**, **[b]**, **[c]**, and **[h]** need to have the ends cut at an angle. Cut the angles according to the list and illustration below.

[a] For the legs, cut a 30° angle each end.
[b] For the middle rail, cut a 5° angle each end.
[c] For the top rail, cut a 5° angle each end.
[h] For the braces, cut a 45° angle each end.

30° angle both ends →

|← 32-3/4" (832 mm) →|

[a] cut 6 pieces

|← 34-3/4" (883 mm) →|

|←25" (635 mm)→|

[h] cut 2 pieces

45° angle both ends

|←34-1/4" (870 mm) →|

[c] cut 3 pieces

5° angle both ends

|————67" (1700 mm)————|

[b] cut 3 pieces

Ready to assemble

At this stage, you should have all the pieces cut as shown below, ready for assembly.

[a] Leg — 6 pieces

[b] Middle rail — 3 pieces

[c] Top rail — 3 pieces

[d] Tabletop board — 9 pieces

[e] Seat board — 6 pieces

[f] Seat cleat — 4 pieces

[g] Table cleat — 2 piece

[h] Brace — 2 pieces

Step 3. Arrange the legs

Lay each pair of legs flat on an even surface, spaced according to the plan drawing below. Use a straight-edge to ensure the bottom of both legs are in-line.

27" (686 mm)

28-3/8" (720 mm)

[a]   [a]

59-5/8" (1516 mm)

straight edge

Straight edge to align the legs to

Step 4. Assemble the frames

Place cross rails **[b]** and **[c]** on legs **[a]** according to the plan drawing below.
Use four 3" (75 mm) screws at each joint, as illustrated in the drawing. Do not place screws in the middle of a joint, as that space is reserved for a bolt.

Screwing

Whenever you're fastening two pieces of wood together with screws, it's important to predrill a **clearance hole** through the top piece.

A **clearance hole** should have the same diameter or slightly larger (but never smaller) than the outside diameter of the screw threads.

This allows the screw to go through the top piece smoothly, with the threads only gripping into the bottom piece, ensuring a tight connection between the two parts.

Clearance hole

Step 5. Stand the frames

Clamp a block flush to the bottom of each leg, as illustrated in the drawing below. This allows the frames to stand by themselves. Hence, you can position the frames and place the boards without needing help from another person to hold the frames upright.

Step 6. Space the frames

Now, space the frames approximately so that when the outer tabletop and seat boards are positioned, they will overhang the frames at each end by 6" (150 mm).

Once the outer boards are placed on, you will be able to adjust the frames accordingly to suit.

Step 7. Put on the outer boards

Only one screw at each joint

Board flush with end of rail

Overhang 6" (150 mm)

Put on the outer boards [explanation]

First, place the outer tabletop and seat boards onto the frame rails, having them overhang each end by 6" (150 mm). Refer to the drawing on this and the previous page for placement. Secure the boards with **only one screw** at each joint - for the time being. A second screw will be added when the frames have been checked square and parallel. Use 3½" (90 mm) screws positioned ⅝" (15 mm) in from the edge of the board.

Is it square and parallel?

LOOKING DOWN VIEW

Carpenters square horizontal check

Carpenters square vertical check

SIDE VIEW

Is it square and parallel? [explanation]

Check that the frames are parallel, and with a carpenter's square ensure the frames are square (at right angles) to the tabletop and seat boards, both horizontally and vertically.
If necessary, make any straightening adjustments, then add a second screw to each joint.
This will hold the unit square while you continue to add the intermediate boards.

Step 8. Add the intermediate boards

Place the intermediate boards. Ensure the ends are flush and the gaps between the boards are even.

Draw a 'screw line ' across the table and seats to keep the screws in a straight line.

Step 9. Attach the cleats

With the table upside-down, screw cleats across the seats and the tabletop, centered between the frames. Use two 3" (75 mm) screws positioned diagonally at each joint.

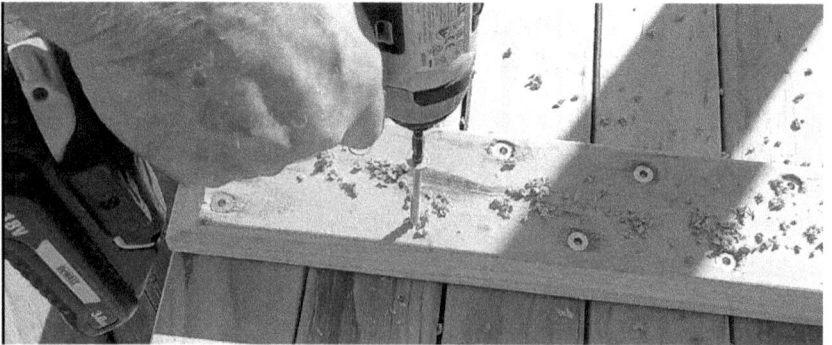

Cleat

Cleat

Step 10. Add the bracing

Ensure the end-frames are square (upright) to the tabletop, and then position each brace as shown in the image below. Screw one end of the brace to the middle rail with two 3" (75 mm) screws, and the other end with 3 screws angled into the tabletop.

Brace

Step 11. Drill and bolt

Drill a bolt hole through the center of every leg and rail joint - twelve altogether.

Insert 1/2" (12 mm) galvanised bolts, add washers and nuts, and tighten them up.

Drill and bolt

Drill and bolt

All finished!

And there it is.

A nice solid, comfortable picnic table that will seat at least eight people.

Build Your Own
Eight-Seater Picnic Table

Using 2 x 6 (50 x 150 mm) lumber

Step-by-step guide

Description

This picnic table is constructed out of 2 x 6 (50 x 150 mm) lumber. It will comfortably seat 8 people. Wide seats positioned both in terms of height and distance from the tabletop ensures easy access and maximum comfort.

Dimensions:
- Length: 8 feet (2.4 meters).
- Width: 67" (1700 mm).
- Height: 29⅞" (758 mm).
- Tabletop width: 34¼" (870 mm).

Part identification

[a] Leg

[b] Middle rail

[c] Top rail

[d] Tabletop board

[e] Seat board

[f] Seat cleat

[g] Table cleat

[h] Brace

[i] Brace support

Plans - Imperial units

Below are the picnic table plans, with dimensions given in inches and fractions of an inch.

Plans - Metric units

Below are the picnic table plans, with dimensions given in millimeters.

About the measurements

Length measurements in this project are provided in both imperial units (inches) and metric units (millimeters).

When measurements are presented side by side, the inch measurements are listed first, followed by the metric equivalents in parentheses.

Length example: 15-3/4" (400 mm).

Size example: 2 x 6 (50 x 150 mm), which means that the wood is 2 inches thick and 6 inches wide, or, in metric terms, 50 millimeters thick and 150 millimeters wide.

Abbreviations:

- ": = inch
- ft: = foot, feet
- mm: = millimeter, millimetre
- m: = meter, metre

Shopping list: Lumber

Wood size	Length	Qty
2 x 6 (50 x 150 mm)	8 ft (2.4 m)	19

The length provided above is a standard stock size, which means it is commonly found at major lumber retailers and home improvement centers. When purchasing select a dressed lumber, which is wood that has been planed (made smooth).

Shopping list: Fixings

Exterior wood screws:

• 106 screws 3" (75 mm) long.

• 60 screws 3½" (90 mm) long.

1/2" (12 mm) galvanized coach/carriage bolts:

• 12 bolts 4" (100 mm) long.

• 12 each nuts and washers to match.

Note: Use the 3" (75 mm) screws for the frames, cleats, and braces.
Use the 3½" (90 mm) screws for the seat boards and the tabletop boards.

Dressed lumber

Dressed lumber is wood that has been planed and smoothed, which makes it smaller than the nominal sizes given.

For example, 2 x 6 (50 x 150 mm) dressed lumber will be 1½" x 5½" (38 x 140 mm) in actual size.

Different countries and regions may have size variations.

The difference in size will not impact the build as it is the lengths of the pieces that are important, not so much the width and thickness of the wood.

Cutting list

2 x 6 (50 x 150 mm) lumber		
Piece ID	**Length**	**Qty**
[a] Leg	36" (912 mm)	6
[b] Middle rail	67" (1700 mm)	3
[c] Top rail	34¼" (870 mm)	3
[d] Tabletop board	8 feet (2.4 m)	6
[e] Seat board	8 feet (2.4 m)	4
[f] Seat cleat	11¼" (285 mm)	4
[g] Table cleat	34¼" (870 mm)	2
[h] Brace	27" (686 mm)	2
[i] Brace support	11¼" (285 mm)	2

INSTRUCTIONS

Start the build

Lets go!

Step 1. Cut all the pieces

Cut all the pieces to the lengths given in the **Cutting list**.

All the pieces can be cut from the standard stock lengths that are listed in the **Shopping list**.

Following on the next page is a **Cutting plan** showing how all the pieces can be cut from the standard lengths of lumber given in the **Shopping list**.

From this

Cut this

Cutting plan

The drawing below illustrates how all the necessary pieces can be cut from nineteen lengths of 2 x 6 lumber, each measuring 8 feet (2.4 m) in length.

The number at the end of each piece indicates the number of repetitions needed for that specific piece.

←————————8 feet (2.4 m)————————→	
d	x 6
e	x 4
a · a · f · f	x 2
a · a · i · i	x 1
b · h	x 2
c · g	x 2
b	x 1
c	x 1

Step 2. Cut the angles

Once all the pieces are cut to length, pieces **[a]**, **[b]**, **[c]**, and **[h]** need to have the ends cut at an angle.

Cut the angles according to the list and drawing below.

[a] For the legs, cut a 30° angle each end.

[b] For the middle rail, cut a 5° angle each end.

[c] For the top rail, cut a 5° angle each end.

[h] For the braces, cut a 45° angle each end.

30° angle both ends

←—32-3/4" (832 mm)—→

[a] cut 6 pieces

←——36" (912 mm)——→

←—27" (686 mm)—→

[h] cut 2 pieces

45° angle both ends

←—34-1/4" (870 mm)—→

[c] cut 3 pieces

5° angle both ends

←———67" (1700 mm)———→

[b] cut 3 pieces

Ready to assemble

At this stage, you should have all the pieces cut as shown below, ready for assembly.

[a]	Leg	6 pieces
[b]	Middle rail	3 pieces
[c]	Top rail	3 pieces
[d]	Tabletop board	6 pieces
[e]	Seat board	4 pieces
[f]	Seat cleat	4 pieces
[g]	Table cleat	2 piece
[h]	Brace	2 pieces
[I]	Brace support	2 pieces

Step 3. Arrange the legs

Lay each pair of legs flat on an even surface, spacing them according to the plan drawing below. Use a straight-edge to ensure the bottom of both legs are in-line.

27" (686 mm)

28-3/8" (720 mm)

[a]   [a]

59-5/8" (1516 mm)

straight edge

Straight edge to align the legs to

Step 4. Assemble the frames

Note: Assemble the frames lying flat on even ground or on top of a suitable work bench.

Place cross rails **[b]** and **[c]** on legs **[a]** according to the plan drawing below.

Use four 3" (75 mm) screws at each joint, as illustrated in the drawing below. Do not place screws in the middle of a joint, as that space is reserved for a bolt.

Screwing

Whenever you're fastening two pieces of wood together with screws, predrill a **clearance hole** through the top piece.

A **clearance hole** should have the same diameter or slightly larger (but not smaller) than the outside diameter of the screw threads.
This allows the screw to go through the top piece smoothly, with the threads only gripping into the bottom piece, ensuring a tight connection between the two parts.

Clearance hole

Step 5. Stand the frames

Clamp a block flush to the bottom of each leg, as illustrated in the drawing below. This will allow the frames to stand by themselves. Hence, you can position the frames and place the boards without needing help from another person to hold the frames upright.

Step 6. Space the frames

Now, space the frames approximately so that when the tabletop and seat boards are positioned, they will overhang the frames at each end by 6 inches (150 mm).

Once the outer boards are placed on, you will be able to adjust the frames accordingly to suit.

Step 7. Put on the outer boards

Only one screw at each joint

Board flush with end of rail

Overhang 6"
(150 mm)

Put on the outer boards [explanation]

First, place the outer tabletop and seat boards onto the frame rails, having them overhang each end by 6" (150 mm). Refer to the drawing on this and the previous page for placement. Secure the boards with **only one screw** at each joint - for the time being. A second screw will be added when the frames have been checked square and parallel. Use 3½" (90 mm) screws positioned ¾" (19 mm) in from the edge of the board.

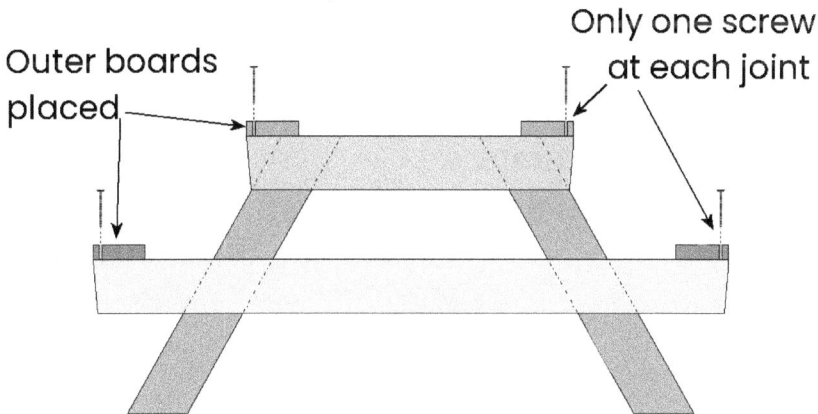

Only one screw at each joint

Outer boards placed

Is it square and parallel?

Check that the frames are square and parallel before adding a second screw at each joint.

LOOKING DOWN VIEW

Carpenters square horizontal check

Carpenters square vertical check

SIDE VIEW

Is it square and parallel? [explanation]

Check that the frames are parallel, and with a carpenter's square ensure the frames are square (at right angles) to the tabletop and seat boards, both horizontally and vertically. If necessary, make any straightening adjustments, then add a second screw to each joint.
This will hold the unit square while you continue to add the intermediate boards.

Step 8. Add the intermediate boards

Place the intermediate boards. Ensure the ends are flush and the gaps between the boards are even.

Draw a 'screw line ' across the table and seats to keep the screws in a straight line.

Step 9. Attach the cleats

With the table upside-down, screw cleats across the seats and the tabletop, centered between the frames. Also attach the brace supports **[i]** as shown in the image below. Use two 3" (75 mm) screws positioned diagonally across each joint.

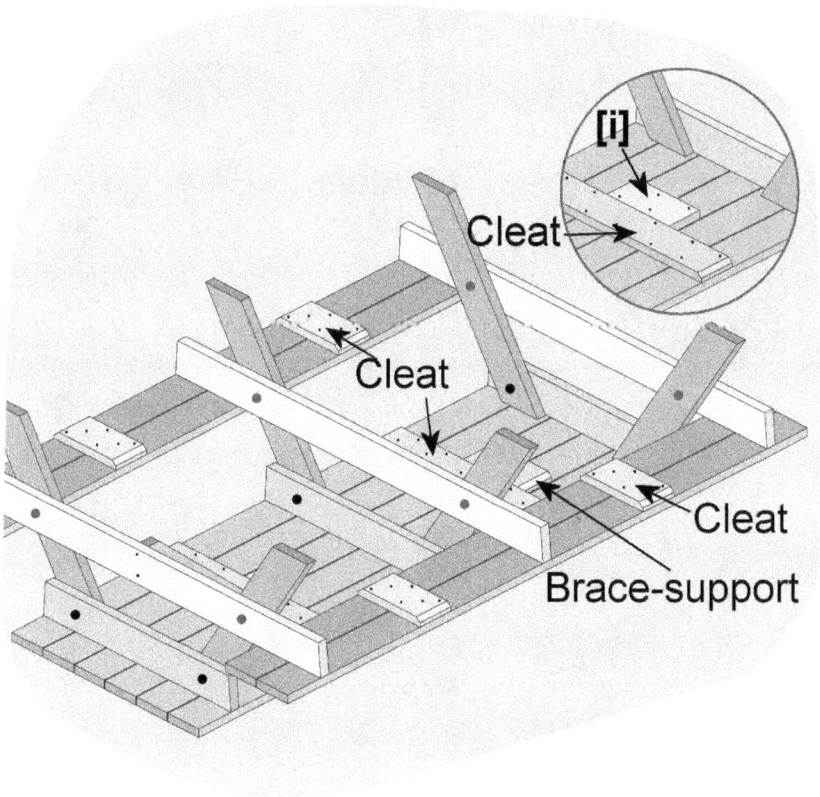

Step 10. Add the bracing

Ensure the end-frames are square (upright) to the tabletop, and then position each brace as shown in the image below. Screw one end of the brace to the middle rail with two 3" (75 mm) screws, and the other end with 3 screws angled into the brace support.

Middle rail

Brace

Brace support

Step 11. Drill and bolt

Drill a bolt hole through the center of every leg and rail joint - twelve altogether.
Insert 1/2" (12 mm) galvanised bolts, add washers and nuts, and tighten them up.

Drill and bolt

Drill and bolt

All finished!

And there it is.

A nice solid, comfortable picnic table that will seat at least eight people.

The Author

Les Kenny has been creating and authoring woodworking projects for many years, with an online presence spanning almost 25 years. Although mostly retired now, he occasionally works on projects and continues to write. Les is a husband, a father of four, and a proud grandfather of seven. You can find his website at leskenny.com.

www.ingramcontent.com/pod-product-compliance
Lightning Source LLC
Chambersburg PA
CBHW071733020426
42331CB00008B/2008